ELEP HANT TACO

AUTHOR BIO

Joe Montaño III is a poet, painter, collage artist, small press owner with his wife Debbie, music nerd, pet parent & a promoter of free thinking through art & poetry. Joe is the author of several other published collections of poetry, including:

Five O'Clock (2016)

California Prayer & Other Poems 2010 – 2016 (2017)

The Half-Breed Horse Thief (2018)

Forthcoming Works of Poetry:

Rock-n-Roll Poems: The LP

For all the weirdos

In memory of Belle

Contents

ELEPHANT TACOS

I Am Told

A coffin made of Earth, I am told
is where the female stink
of soil, worms & feathers in a hell
of animal doom I can bury my black
spun heart.

I am told
that I don't have to die
here in a hallway of burning
toys & false memories.

Stainless, not made
of the chalky
touches from childhood idiots
on my creaky body.

I am told that I am tall, that I am
mean, that I am an elephant reeking
of flower-boy tacos & suburban
white trash.

And I am cruel, to the breasts of my Love,
to the mind of my Love.

I am as deaf as a sunflower,
bleeding like a black stone.
My rage is frail under
Earth's womanly
grasp.

Elephant Taco

My skin is free
of criminals, but not
undone by hate.
A wax cut out actor,
I-talian playing a Mexican junkie
anti-hero.

Losing my belief
in Earth and her long
whispered knowledge,
and the breath of light
that mutes my pain.

My heart & body pulsate thought.
I am closer to death,
closer to life,
remembering my breath in the trees
of youth in new morning.

We didn't know.
We ain't been schooled.
We did not learn it.
We have the Spanish Blues.

Children speaking no Spanish,
a little bit lucky, but a bit like
Elvis' Blues, or Picasso's stolen
African masks.

Shamed by our name, behind
a grey memory with a sleepless
sigh, I spell my name for idiots,
each letter like a number.

The Spanish Blues,
our grandparents stole
the land & crops of our tongues.
Spanish Blues, it's in the blood.

Shame & taboo
splinter, and we can dance in feathers,
all the men are allowed.
Awkward bodies vibrate the room
in bleeding & loving.

The children
of the jungle,
of boyhood,
and the girl's
touch and
breath.

I miss my few
childhood friends.
Rain colored children
with crooked smiles,
tall tales, shitty parents.

Their perverted eyes
reflecting a dim future.
Wind worn coins in their hands,
as they whisper in alleyways.

I miss them for the children
that they were, not who they have become.
I see them running inside the dark,
tainted before first kisses.

The Gift of Anger

My thinking heart
in rhythm with
grunt-grunt songs of men,
their crude tongues
of primitive origin.

Caressing my knuckle scars,
fondling sexy scales, my friends were
toothy-fish-boys.
I seaweed strangled
myself.

A new breath, releasing
sea scum foaming from my mouth.

Cold & ancient. A confused
dreamy hate. Old & forgotten,
a junkie's runny nose,
silence in the bell echo-hall.
No one says a name.

The gift of anger
is handmade, seedless,
rotted by brutality.

The sun is waiting with all his teeth blaring
beyond the filthy surface.

Yellow Light of Confidence

I am a child with his scars
of quietude, and fear
of speaking with love in his
shameless voice.

Dead lungs,
wickedness & confusion.
Air is stagnant before
radical movement, in the coolness
of the fall.

I live inside the silver light
of forgiveness.

In yellow lights of confidence,
I tell mom&dad about The Underneath
of the bed, and the stains of timeless childhood.

My chest & head free of memories.
I cheer the wicked death of nostalgia.

The child stood there always,
frozen with his winter hate, hot sounds
tongued lashed at my face.
Speaking endlessly, secrets & pain from the dusty floor.

The skank scent of elephant rot
on my lips.
Love is wrapped sloppily
in seaweed rope, shells strung
across the knot.

The sorrows of the aging
head & body & self,
quiet with tiny surprises
that we must bleed.

The gift of love
is fragments of a sand dollar broken
by time, we cradle in our hands
and blow at with our ragged breath.

Foggy morning laziness
through us,

calm touch
and the day is nothing,

timeless, slow.

We walk to anyplace
along the water's edge,

as if we were speaking
in accidents that this place
understands, and not us.

And the gift hurts,
as we sift sand into milk.

New bird truces & delights, & free
of utopias. I'd rather reside in a cool
silent room of ideas.

New,
clear & deliberate,
a speckling of leaf shadowed lite
decorates over me.

Inside the thicket of trees,
my body does not feel pain.
Wishes, expectations dissipate
thru the blaze of sunlight weaving
fragments of thin-light-calmness.
I forget my sentiments for pain, my
comfort in pale, confused mornings.

Silent.
Asking nothing.
Saying nothing.
Seeing in the haze my worn-out clothes
hanging lame in the trees.

Free from old frail bones dusted
onto the pavement.
I see the years coming quicker.
I continue waking slowly into the trees.

Coded tongue, like that of white-boys.
No silly smiles in your belly.
A tight uniform of tough-guy.
Rituals of stupidity, a soldier,
unpaid pawn.

I am not the brute boy you require of me
for your simple soul & religion.

Don't call me to your deaths.
You are a coward & a killer, and there
is nothing weird about you.
No flower-less brown boy death logic
with dead pigeons makes you earthly.

Caveman don't call me to your violence.
Death threats & caskets closing, I can take a punch
as my ghost exits my eyes.

You tell me I am sugar, salt and cracked concrete.
You tell me my abstractions are too high for your education.
But you are a whore of tradition, drunk & slave collecting
like a Conquistador popping white-trash opioids.

Don't call to me my name
with your limp numb tongue.

No More Heroes

Whiskey stains dried into wooden flesh.
Some men are like ancient tables.

The women left days ago.
The violence & spite were not youthful gestures.
Our bodies kicked & sprawled at nothing.

Boredom & importance, and the lashing out occurs.

Dying in ugly vanity & sadness, nested
in the primitive bird tangles of vacant lots
and crumbled bricks.

We have become our own Cutters,
yelling, destroying for our lonesome
nasty selves.

Lost in candy wrappers & addictions & ass
& careless choosing of leaders.

I no longer feel dead inside. I no longer have heroes.

Of Primitive Man

I have covered my body
with feathers of mud,
with fleeting pain,
and bird carcasses
disappearing in exhale,

beaks scatter across my bare toes,
talons are whispery husks.

Mud on my face,
a primitive man, not wanting to die
in this decade of idiocy,
in this overcrowded city.

Ego, anger behind windows & doors.
But fruit alive in the trees.
The hangman's knot has rotted,
shotgun is rusted, and the sneak's
razor has been found.

Creep

A sleepy fog of daydream horrors.
I end this darkness.
I am a naïve Creep,
picking teeth, nose, butt,
no one stands next to me
as I rot.

I am to blame for the burnt
chairs in this cruel yard.

I hide out, pin-picking my flesh
to forget the rage & chaos
of dreams.

Muscles pulled, the quiet
hate, exhausted from when I was
the boy killed in the woods.

The call of wild boys,
dead awakening in their howls,
careless touching.
Their bodies dripping wet with awful killing,
their hands versed well in quietness.

Her losses of love

are ceramic

birds

limping across the tops

of hot walls

of concrete

death, watching

baby chicks falling

from burning nests.

The Cruel Men

1.

In a dank
misty church corridor,
little
men
whisper, in manifest destiny, in fear,

for God is a drunk fat white man
living in his mom's basement.
He is amazingly American & simply mediocre,
burning children's toys,
fantasy warpaint on his face.

The cruel men,

ignorant, graceless beasts,

in a long line, angrily shuffling
towards old age and their God's insults,
their minds broken, bodies tangled, and staring into black
distance into a mirror of their ugly faces.

And their faces are without breath, as if madmen
screaming, foaming at the gate of paradise.

2.

Pouring rancid milk over their faces,
to be unblinded, this race of the stupid
is killing us all, just for a minor victory,
these children with meat in their teeth.

Hunger for kingdom, to feel ignorant
in the gut,
to feed the hole in the head.

The starvation of many is calculated,

and should be questioned,
for meaning,
for purpose,
for the scars on children.

The American man is a savage
of a nothing diet, an empty feast
of nonsense words,
dumb as iron, standing naked, covered
in blood and milk, in front of wives,
daughters and lovers.

3.

A father's anger spit across the room,
jawbone and hands ache in familiar
youthful memories.

The family curse,
a long static, chilly street
of crooked hearts of dumb men,
lost in prostitutes & boyhood.

Wicked and distrusting
their own minds & dreams,
the cruel men claw at the soft
hands of mothers.

With neither gifts of love nor
anger, but stoic control, and
a dangerous demise.

Cursed, slowly they become unseen,
unloved as they die of the wounds of fantasy.

A fore-fathers' exit,
petty & killing, the evil cycle
of men dancing around the fires
of their own boats.

The guilty in their boyhood sorrows,
collecting all their revenge tactics, building
their plans to get away with it all.

Part One

(An improv. poem based on
a hypnoses therapy session)

Red.
Orange.
Yellow.
Green.
Blue.
Purple.

Breathing
w/
Earth…body
curving softly
with movement
of trees.

I walk
into a forest
like floating
in a dream.

Fog lifts, fades
with snaky gestures
of arrogance.

(childlike).

Deep pine scents.
Sweet shit dirt stench.
Naked & pretty, I walk
further into the cool
mean
trees.

Achy
Nitemare
Visions
&
Horrid
Morning
Chatter, & a
Fright in mouth,
I am free of them all.

Aging body.
My crooked leg.
My crooked teeth.
My curved spine,
I exit my body.

Pain
fades
under
the shiny
command of
red.

New breath,
slow dance
of touch.

New
Breath,

orange
in a waterfall
glow.

Breath,
and to
yellow

washing obsessions
away thru neon-flow.

Then to
green,
jungle leaves,
emerald pea plant
light transforming
pain thru wild
young
exhales.

And then to
blue,
bright & guiding
patchwork of
complex Blues
swerving,
cleaving
thru breath.

Shame & anger
from my brow, neck,
bones, from my head,
my mind. Slow breaths,
free of reward & dust.
I breathe.

Then to
purple,

calm waters,
soft moon eyes,
compassion
behind a peeling purple door,
purple
in sea & soil
leaf & paper.

I breathe,
new breath,

Red.
Orange.
Yellow.
Green.
Blue.
Purple.

Part Two

(An improv. poem based on
a hypnoses therapy session)

Breathing.
Humming.
Awake.
Breathing.

Eyes closed.
Light swallows my body.
Head murmurs
with unfamiliar
silence.

Soft,
old
humming
replaces the static.

I breathe
in bright
colors.

Deep,
in & out
thru the nose.

I breathe pain
away, to smile
at fear, to be naked
with the world.

I breathe,
double me away,
triple me away,
from ego, from

memories.

Eyes closed,
I walk in the woods,
breathing
the strangeness of
earth.

I breathe
and not afraid
to be alive.
I breath for the dead
bird inside me.

Breathing.
Releasing.
Breathing.
Releasing.

Free of horror, of
fear, of saints, demons,
and superstition.

I breathe,
free of dreams,
of shadows.

Breathing.
Releasing.

Free of scar tissue,
blood-clots, free of
false memories.

Free of
moss, vines
at my lungs, my limbs.

Free of feeling
unworthy.
Free of being
ashamed.
Free of the moss of
hate.
Free of death.

I breathe.
I am a speck
of dirt.
I release.
I am a fly at a dead
cow's belly.
I breathe.
I am a wildflower.
I release.

Humming.
Awaking.
Breathing.

The scent of raw pine.
I look to the treetops.
Yellow calms me.
Purple opens me.
I breathe.

Wild seed grit
on my face.
I breathe.
Citrus smells in the air.
I release.
I breathe.
I release.
I breathe.
I release.
I open my eyes.

1.

A new life,
a new breath,
a new meditation,
takes courage
to enter.

It is unusual,
like life & youth
have always been,
with humanity in waiting.

Catching my breath,
is what I do, catching
it & being aware of it.

In silence
or in humming,
thru forests of the cool now.

Breathing. Smiling.
Walking thru the tangle
of winds & limbs, whipping
insects into a choir.

2.

Seeds of suffering
are watered with just a few words,
when young.

Continued into the years,
weeds tangle where flowers
could have grown, suffocating
where breath should strive.

Without blame, hate, & pain we
move towards the freedom we
have always possessed in the calming
of our breathing.

Seeds of suffering
need not be the origin of our words,
and free of the tangles of blame, the wicked
teeth of hate, we move towards
the silence of calm heartbeats.

THE ROCK-N-ROLL POEMS: THE L.P.

Many moments when R-n-R
laid a tender joke on us all, loud
with goddesses and
in halls of velvet, telling us lies
like, youth is timeless.

A ragged Lord, confused Saints and Ghosts,
St. Christopher & Eros & Nero, so archaic
in their armored myth skin, loveless romances
spun quickly as black vinyl.

Smothered in the embraces of midnite women
half darkened by the dying age of excess.
Smothered in the hugs of Bolan's Revolution.

Dying with the grey wings & rotting leaves of overdose,
no halos above rock stars heads,
and there is no glory
to pretend.

Smothered in the embrace of old age
and smothered in love and not a strut,
fighting for the smart girl not the pistol shooter.
Smothered in my pain, in my hips, my head,
and in the decay of iron & wood.

A Memphis Punk Rocker
(In Memory of Jay Reatard)

Junker low on gas,
breaking strings in a temper tantrum,
drunk, peeling dark eyelash-sadness
from your face.

Remembering a strange place for
a short time, death was shaken away
and the struggle of the riot
was lost in the long dying of trees,

with Rock and Roll
as vital as Poetry.

We admit the bastard that it is, with itchy
blankets & flesh.

We shake away the death mites & fleas,
who ignore all the dogs and go for our frail
guitar player, and we are unable to save him
from the alleyways.

The steam of a breath kills the candles, stiffens
the horse hairs and drowns the gasping lungs.

When Neko Case Haunted Our House

A gasp of Latin air, a warm tongue spoken, the drums
beat us a quiet melancholy rhythm
our blood flows beastly for.

We test the atmosphere and try not to die
from a simple line that dissolves
the World's viscous grey ways.

We confess nothing to the window,
for it no longer says our faces in dew
or fog or rain.

She bathed us in the rabbit hairs,
dried our faces as we cried for each
other when the darkness said too much,
and darkness said too much.

Phantom gone, and a woman writes
the book on us. We dust our frames, we remain
silent in the hell of words.

And she haunted, and we never knew, we
never knew, we were too late
to see her move the books & chairs.

When Neko Case was playing loudly in our house,
she didn't scold us or steal our bread,
she moved the clock to the drawer, she moved
the darkness that spoke too much, and it was dark
for much too long.

An Unknown Soldier (In Memory of Fred Cole)

Spinning the black from an old machine,
no one tells the romantic pirate how to make
a sound, how the groove cuts the skin with what
size blade.

Rock-n-Roll often makes soldiers, welders,
teachers, sailors, pic-pockets, janitors
out of her kids.
A paperless job where the sound
is falling from ancient oak of beat up
guitars in young hands.

Underground in the Oregon woods,
guitars ringing a buzz-saw sound or a sludge
of rained-down strings.
I get lost and talk to drunks of the thicket,
punks of the street corner & alleyways.

Everywhere the sound of music is lacing
a crude memory thru the black dots of poetry
on sunburnt pages.

The unknown soldier shows me his dusty cabin
full with RnR history, a hearse where rare 7 inch records
go to die, and a faded music sheet with the real words
to "Louie, Louie" scrawled on it.

With his Love, strong in doorway telling her
own stories of days of denim & leather & cold vans
with no heat & candy-bar dinners.
The vicious dream
we poets weave our fur thru.
The angry love of midnite souls afraid of the day-job,
we are falling apart in the chaos but never far
from our dusty homes, our halos fading,
and our breath of the new-born.

A Serious Case of Bad Brains

She's wearing cat-eyes, purple
pink hair, tiny tattoos that offend
up close, cut up rags
and she smells like weed & fruit
candies.

I spilt my beer
and the band sucked tonite.
My sick mind & body survived the ashy
air and chlorine bathtub, and the sweet
cowardice of most men I know and
see.

She moves with a serious case of Bad Brains,
her quiet songs of terror
are aching every stich & bone. Her maddening
hands flex and contort, her feet pound the floor
with a drummer's heaviness.

She has a small apartment with books, art things,
a bong and pillows all over the floor. She has me
here now, shy & buzzed, she puts on some ole
Rock Steady, and we dance, shushed in the loud bass
drums and gits…and we die, then play a card game,
then she reads my tarot, and I believe her and we sleep
in the Christmas lights left-on-all-day.

Zeus of Dayton
(A Tribute to Robert Pollard)

Like Joan of Arc or a gang of bloody winged
sparrows, the voices rang true and loud:
the hungry dream-makers
play the games of phantoms in the hallways,
backyards and basements.

How do we explain the moments of genius-electricity
that ignites then dies a miserable death at our feet?

If airplanes were our trustiest birds
we might be able to never really feel
the ground bite us and anchor our better bodies.
Speaking to myself and thinking alone,
fearful and shamed in the company of others,
my music is a box of years, a box of toy soldiers
sacrificed to a bloody hill.

The Zeus of Dayton is in the classroom,
The no-hitter, the only RnR reality. Teacher mugshot,
a no smile, fear and nowhere-ness, not yet born is
the king of cassette tapes.

We are waiting for the original monk to leave
his self exile in the basement.
No parental permission or favor from the wife,
the Failure can no longer wait by the fence.

The Heavy Metal Kids are making fun of our wizard,
& we don't care, we don't know them,
& we are waiting, cold & wild, but quietly,
waiting for lightening bolts to fall from the clouds.

199andSomething Forever
(A Tribute to Guided By Voices)

It's cold and we move as fast as
starved kids can go. It's lonesome in the class
rooms as we find the misfits in their fake
fur coats, long hair and their weirdo gazes
full of questions & secrets.
It's easy being young when wisdom's
horrors are yet to be uncensored.

We write shitty poems in youth.
We find each other by being gentle in our rudeness.
Warmth we crave as no one should be alone when
this hungry & young.
Music & books of poetry we find
in odd, crammed bookshops.

Its 199somethingand5 every night, the sad
sunset when leaving your love at their doorway,
the mist under the red, the softness above us all,
the dying of teenage memories as we burn wings
and dismiss dreams, and gather our socks & shoes,
for the cold is an awful hurt.

199somethingand6 and we are afraid to look at each
other in the noon sparkle. No longer embarrassed by youth
but the movements of grown-ups and who we never
could be. We didn't plan to fail our parents, but we did
it with the style of cosmonauts in torn sweaters and jeans.
I grew to love them all, all the friends and the vanishing
acts they pulled without lying or spitting teeth in vengeance
at the evil of men.

We love them, the gang
of dirty haired girls so lovely
in autumn, when dying has no say
on the young and their loud music.

    We hurt a little more as the year ends
    and a new one begins.
    All the bands are disappearing
    or becoming myths.
    We don't know these new kids
    and the safety they desire.

Dirty haired girls, porcelain and dizzy
with the wisdom of dark times in the muted
lights turning from red-green-blue.

    We hurt less as age calms that nostalgic insect
    and the generation gap never
    was and we gather with less of a crowd and the dirty
    haired girls are all married now.